To my Yeska:

_____

With love from:

_____

Contents

Christian Media Publishers,
PO Box 4502, Durbanville, 7551
www.christianmediapublishing.com

Author: Ewald van Rensburg

Illustrations, Design & Layout: Lilani Brits

Publishing Project Manager: Noeline N Neumann

Reg No 2010/008573/07

Text: Maranatha Publishing: Used by kind agreement.

Printed in Malaysia through PrettyInPress Productions.

First Editon, second printing, 2013
ISBN 978-1-920460-49-5

CMP-kids books have been developed with your child's
developmental phases and unique temperament in mind.
For a full explanation of the **unique temperament** and **developmental
phases** icons visit the CMP website **www.cmpublishing.co.za**

YesKids

Bible Stories

- about Prayer -

Kids saying YES! For Prayer

Written by Ewald van Rensburg
Illustrations by Lilani Brits

christian media publishing

pointing children in the **right direction**

1. God hears when you pray

(1 Samuel 1)

Elkanah and his wife Hannah lived in a small village. The people of the village teased Hannah because she could not have children. This made her very unhappy.

Hannah prayed in the temple that God would give her a baby. She cried while she prayed.

Eli, the priest, saw her crying and he thought she was drunk. He scolded her. But when she told him her story he realised that she was not drunk. She was just very, very sad.

So Eli said to her, "God will give you a baby." And it happened just as Eli said it would. The baby was born and they called him Samuel.

God was good to Hannah, because after Samuel she had another five children. And nobody ever teased her again.

Come, let's pray together:

Thank you, Jesus, that
you always hear my prayers.
Amen.

2. Speak Lord, I am listening!
(1 Samuel 3)

Early one morning something special happened to Samuel. He was living with Eli in the temple, but Eli was still asleep. A voice called, "Samuel!"
Samuel answered, "I'm coming!"

Quickly he ran to Eli. "You called me. Here I am," he said to the sleepy Eli. Eli shook his head. "I didn't call you," he said. When it happened a second time, Eli realised that it was God who was calling Samuel. So Eli said to Samuel, "The next time someone calls your name, say 'Speak Lord, I'm listening.' "

This is exactly what Samuel did, and the Lord spoke to him.

9

He would remember it until the day he died. From that day on everybody talked about Samuel, who always did what the Lord asked him to do.

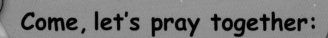

Come, let's pray together:

Lord Jesus, help me always listen to the things you say to me in the Bible. Amen.

These days the Lord talks to us through the Bible.

3. Wise King Solomon

(1 Kings 3)

One night King Solomon dreamed that God asked him, "What is the one thing you want the most from me?"
"Help me to make wise choices," Solomon answered. So God made Solomon the wisest person in the whole world.

One day two women came to see King Solomon. They brought a baby with them. Each of the women said the baby was hers.

One woman's baby had died in the night, so she had stolen the other woman's baby. But which woman was telling the truth? Who was the real mother?

Solomon made a clever plan. "Cut the baby in half." he said. "Then each of you will get half a baby."

Straight away one woman said, "Yes, cut him in half." But the other woman said, "No, please, rather give the baby to her. Just don't kill him."

Solomon immediately knew the second woman was the real mother, because she really cared about the baby. So he gave the baby to her.

 Everybody talked about his great wisdom.

Come, let's pray together:

Jesus, help me to bring you joy every day by listening to you. Amen.

Remember to pray every day.

4. Daniel in the Lion's Den
(Daniel 6)

Daniel was a very important Jew who lived in Persia. Everyone knew how much he loved God. He prayed three times every day. Some people were jealous of him, so they told King Darius to make a new law saying people could only pray to the king, not to God.

Anybody who disobeyed that law would be thrown to the lions. Daniel did not care about the new law. He carried on praying to God as usual: morning, noon and evening.

The jealous people told the king that Daniel was breaking the law.

So Daniel was thrown into a den filled with lions. God closed the lions' mouths and Daniel was safe. Then the king knew that Daniel's God was the only true God.

Come, let's pray together:

Jesus, my life
is safe in your hands.
Amen.

God can help you too, just as he helped Daniel in the lion's den.

19

5. Jesus visits the temple

(Luke 2)

Jesus was growing up nicely.
He always listened to his parents.

One day Mary, Joseph and Jesus travelled to Jerusalem. They went to a festival with all the other Jews to praise God for his greatness.

After the festival Joseph and Mary were on their way home when they made a terrible discovery:
Jesus was missing!

They looked everywhere for him, but Jesus was not with the other children who were part of the group of travellers. Mary and Joseph were so worried. They hurried back to Jerusalem to look for Jesus.
They searched all over the big city ...

At last they found Jesus. He was in the temple. They were so happy to find him. He was busy talking to the clever men about God. The clever men were amazed to hear how much Jesus knew about God.

Back home in Nazareth the people knew that God loved Jesus, and they also loved Jesus very much.

Come, let's pray together:

Jesus, I want to be
just like you.
Amen.

Your parents care for you just as Jesus' parents cared for him.

Guidelines for parents

Faith Icon

The formation of faith is indeed unique to each child; there are however general characteristics which apply to all children. There are three main ways that children develop faith:

- Parents regularly reading the Bible, telling Bible and other faith based stories, praying together and doing faith building activities with their children (such as the ones found in this book).
- Children ask questions – parents need to take these questions seriously and answer them according to the child's level of understanding.
- Children follow the example of those caring for them.

Emotional intelligence icon

We experience emotions long before we learn the language to be able to express how we are feeling. Therefore it is important that children are taught to verbalise what they are feeling. Use the illustrations accompanying the stories and ask your child how they think the people or animals in the picture feel. This helps them become aware of their own emotions as well as those of others. It provides a learning opportunity where the child can learn appropriate words to express how they are feeling.

Reading icon

A wonderful world opens up for your child when they start learning to read. Enjoy every moment of this exciting adventure with your child. Let them sit on your lap where they can be comfortable and feel safe and secure. Open the book holding it so that you can both see the pages. Read clearly and with enthusiasm. As you know you can read the same story over and over. Point out where you are reading with your finger as you go along. This will help your child to begin to see the relationship between letters, sounds, words and their meaning. Encourage your child's attempts at reading – even of it sounds like gibberish.

Listening skills icon

Listening is an important learning and development skill. You can help develop this skill in your child by encouraging them to listen attentively, and understand what they are hearing. Let them look at the illustrations and then use their imagination to tell the story back to you in their own words. You can also encourage them to do this by asking questions relating to the story. Yet another way is to leave out words from a story the child knows well and let them fill in the missing words.

Vocabulary icon

Use every opportunity to build your child's vocabulary – it is a lifelong gift which you are giving to them. Start with everyday objects and people in the illustrations in books. Point at the picture, say the word, form a short sentence using the word. Repeat it again and then let your child say the word. Try to use the word in another context – if there is a tent in the picture you are looking at then say: we sleep in a tent when we go camping.

Numeracy skills icon

It is important for your child develop numeracy skills. Play simple games such as: "How many ducks are there in the picture? If we add two more ducks how many are there now? Then if three fly away? (use your fingers to illustrate this) How many are left? They also need to recognise the shape of numbers – cut large numbers from cardboard – let your child play with these – place the numbers in order forming a line from one to ten.